Welcome to Practical Kindness!

Welcome!

This book provides an easy way to incorporate compassion, courage, and kindness into your life. It has 4 key sections, and every week provides a different, easily-digestible focus.

We begin with the foundation: Self-Kindness. Your first 12 weeks will focus on key components such as how you speak to yourself, setting boundaries, becoming your own best friend, and more.

The second section builds on your foundation and dives into the Courage to be Imperfect. For these 11 weeks, you'll be inspired to start small, love your process, and give yourself some credit!

Section 3 has tips for Kind Living. From weeks that help you on holidays to connecting through conversations, these 10 weeks help you live a kinder life.

Finally, we round out the year with 19 weeks of Life Lessons. Hope, integrity, and growth are just some of the topics you'll dig into in this section.

Get ready to have your kindest year yet! Mix and match the weeks, skip around, stay focused on 1 area for a month, if it feels right for you. There's no wrong way to use this book, and it's one that you'll find yourself reaching for time and time again.

www.KindOverMatter.com

Table of Contents

www.KindOverMatter.com

SECTION 1: Foundations of Self-Kindness

www.KindOverMatter.com

Week 1: How Self-Kindness Can Change the World

Push, push, push. Go, go, go. These are the messages the world gives us. If you just push harder, do more and sleep less, you'll go further. We're taught this is how to get ahead and it's just what you have to do, but we're never taught how to be happy.

We live in the most unhealthy, medicated society on record, and I don't think that's a coincidence. I believe there is a direct correlation between the messaging we hear and our (lack of) health, joy and happiness.

What does being kind to yourself have to do with any of this? The answer is capacity.

When you're so busy running around pushing harder and doing more and going further, you have very limited capacity. Our culture glorifies being busy and we wear the label as a badge of honor, but the truth is, this constant state of busy-ness keeps us stuck in the cycle of being stressed out, angry and resentful…and nobody is changing the world from that place.

Maybe you're feeling motivated to be politically involved. Maybe you want to volunteer at your local animal shelter. Maybe you want to mentor young kids with limited resources.

Whatever you want to do, if you try adding 1 more thing to your stressed-out life, it is not going to go well. You need capacity to change the world, and you need self-kindness to increase your capacity.
Being kinder to yourself includes things like ensuring you get enough rest, fueling your body with foods that work for you and moving your body in a way that's accessible. It also includes setting boundaries, opening your mind, speaking kindly to yourself and leaning
on the folks who are closest to you.

These acts of self-kindness create capacity. Instead of feeling like you're running on empty all the time, you'll start to notice a feeling of ease and freedom coming back into your days.

Your capacity will return and you'll be able to do the world-changing things you desire.

Week 2: When Self-Kindness is Hard

"Some of the biggest acts of self-kindness are very difficult to do."

What do you think of when you think about self-kindness? Maybe you think about getting more rest or making time to slow down; maybe you picture the stereotypical self-care image of a candlelit bubble bath (which, by the way, is a totally awesome thing to do for yourself!).

Those are all great ways to be kind to yourself, and if you're reading them and getting that longing feeling, please pick one and make it happen this week!

I'm betting that the things you thought about felt easeful in some way. Fantastic! More often than not, we don't allow ourselves to do things that bring more ease into our lives, so that's a great way to start to be kinder to yourself. Those are some of the ways that I started being kinder to myself. When I was feeling super burned out and continuing to add more and more things to my life, many of those things helped get me unstuck.

What about the things that, although they're hard choices, are still acts of self-kindness? I'm talking about having the difficult conversation with a partner, boss, colleague or loved one; saying "no" to the person who is taking advantage of you; walking away from relationships that don't feel good. Some of the biggest acts of self-kindness are very difficult to do in the moment, but they're the right long-term choice.

Next time you come across one of those choices that feels almost impossible in the moment, think about it through the lens of long-term self-kindness. It might not make the action any easier, but it will certainly help you remember the reason why you're doing it.

Week 3: Freedom is the Path, not the Destination

"Freedom was never a destination, it was a path I'd been walking."

I regularly refer to myself as a tightly wound woman. I like things to go a certain way. I like order and schedules and timeliness. Over the years I've relaxed significantly, starting with giving myself a break from my perfectionist expectations and then relaxing in other areas of my life as well. It's not the end of the world if my home isn't perfectly tidy. The friend I'm meeting for coffee won't hate me if I'm 5 minutes late. I'm allowed to rest even if my task list isn't complete.

I used to think that I was working toward something – freedom, for lack of a better word.

Freedom was even one of my Core Desired Feelings. (If you're not familiar with Danielle LaPorte's Desire Map – it rocks!) It was a way I wanted to feel, a place I wanted to reach.
What I didn't realize was that the little things I'd been doing, the little gifts of self-kindness I'd been giving myself – those were all parts of freedom. It was never a destination, it was a path I'd been walking.

Having this realization gave me the power to choose more freedom.

Every time I forgive myself or someone else, that's freedom. Every time I choose my health (physical, mental, spiritual), that's freedom. Every time I speak kindly to myself, that's freedom.

These little ways of choosing how I want to feel have made a big difference. They've lead to bigger shifts, more clarity and more courage. Instead of constantly trying to achieve freedom (or whatever the equivalent desire is for you), I've found it in small, everyday
ways.

Give this a try this week. Maybe you identify with the desire for freedom. Maybe your destination is confidence or clarity or calm. Whatever it is, look for ways you're already there. Find them. Own them. Let yourself feel empowered to choose more of them and
watch what happens.

Week 4: Becoming Your Own Best Friend

There is no one who you will spend more time with than yourself. How does that statement feel? Maybe it feels daunting, or perhaps joyful. It probably depends on how you're feeling about yourself in this particular moment…kind of like your relationship with your best friend.

Often when people think about becoming their own best friend they think it's supposed to be sunshine and roses all the time; but that's simply not reality. I know that I've had moments with my best friend where I've wanted nothing more than some time apart! This is all a part of healthy relationships, yet when it comes to our relationship with ourselves we set these unreasonably high expectations.

Is it awesome to be with yourself some days and you walk around feeling like you rock? Absolutely!

Are there some days when you feel like you want to crawl out of your skin and can't stand to be around yourself? Yup, those days happen, too.

Recognizing this is key. There's nothing wrong with you if you feel frustrated with yourself sometimes. It's not normal to not be in love with yourself at every minute of every day. You're not supposed to always be overjoyed with yourself.

Like any other relationship, the relationship you have with yourself will have its ups and downs. If you build that relationship on a solid foundation of trust, forgiveness, self-kindness, compassion and courage, you're creating a something that will last for the long haul.

Week 5: When to Walk Away

My mom is a huge Kenny Rogers fan, and some of my earliest memories are going to Kenny Rogers concerts with her! As a kid, his song The Gambler was my favorite. The chorus of that song is, "You've got to know when to hold 'em and know when to fold 'em; know when to walk away and know when to run." and while the song is about an old
Texas gambler, that refrain is some pretty solid life advice!

I've got relationships on my mind a lot lately because they shape so much of our human experience. Whether it's having a challenging coworker, a rough spot with your partner or a disagreement with friends, relationships have a big impact on how you feel.

As a kind person you may be more likely to hold on to some relationships for longer than you desire. I've been there and I know it's not always easy to walk away, even when you know it's time to fold 'em.

Let's do a simple, gentle exercise to start choosing people who make you feel good and allocating your time accordingly. Grab a sheet of paper and draw a line down the middle. On the Left side, write the names of folks who make you feel super awesome and loved-up when you're with them. On the Right side, write the names of other folks who you spend time with, but who don't give you that lovin' feeling.

Now, we'll take that a step further. Look at the folks on the right side of your page. Those are the folks who don't make you feel awesome when you spend time with them. Some of the people on that list might be ones you want to keep around but in a much more limited capacity, but I'm betting some of those people are ones you'd like to walk away from.

ENTER THE INNER CRITIC! "You're mean if you don't keep them in your life. What if you hurt their feelings? You should just keep seeing them and suck it up."

Any of that sound familiar???

I know it feels like that inner critic voice is telling you the truth. This week I want to invite you to challenge that voice. Whatever it says, whether it's one of the examples above or something else; instead of taking that voice as fact, pause for a moment and question it. Ask
yourself if it's really true. Is it really true that you're mean if you distance yourself from someone who doesn't feel good to be with? Is it really true that you'll hurt their feelings? Do you have evidence of that? Is it really true that you need to go through life "sucking it
up" in places that don't work?

Challenging that inner critic voice and beginning to choose the people you surround yourself with is a giant act of self-kindness! Setting boundaries around how you want to be treated, how you want to use your time & energy and asking for what you need is a courageous plunge into self-kindness…and hey, if you don't want to take my word for it, take Kenny's.

Week 6: You are Flawed...and Worth Loving

This one is for you if you feel like showing your flaws will make you unlovable.

She came to me with a laundry list of her personal flaws and mistakes. Her professional confidence was shaken to the core and she didn't know how to stop putting pressure on herself and feeling overwhelmed. Her flaws were the only thing she could see, and that clouded vision was impacting every area of life. Through her eyes, everyone else's life was shiny and together while hers was a chaotic mess. It was getting difficult for her to believe that she was lovable.

On the outside you'd never know she was feeling this way. She was a seasoned professional in a prestigious field, she had a home, a partner, a circle of friends and an active social life...but she didn't believe any of that was real. She was paralyzed by the idea of sharing her flaws with friends or her partner...which is exactly where we started.

There were no big risks or scary instructions or tough love moments. Our first step was simply to amp up the self-kindness. We explored the places that made her feel good, the activities that brought her joy and I gave her full permission to spend as much time on those things as possible. Then we moved on to her inner voice and I learned how she spoke to herself. Like most of us, it was pretty unkind, so we explored some techniques to reframe that inner voice. She gradually started feeling like the ground underneath her was more solid. The awareness of her flaws was still there but she could also see her lovability again.

When the time was right we took a big step and I invited her to ask someone she loves what they love about her. (You should know that this is one of my FAVORITE things to ask my clients to do...and you can totally do this for yourself. I promise you'll get a huge boost if you want to give it a try!)

You see, we all feel unsteady from time to time. Even the most confident among us loses our footing and starts to worry that we really are unlovable. Having a reminder of the things that someone important loves about us is a great way to ground yourself back in your lovability when things feel unsteady.

Week 7: There is No Algorithm for Joy

"Her feelings were not even on her radar."

"I wish there was just an algorithm I could use to decide," she said when thinking about who to invite to a special event. "If I invite X, then I have to invite Y." This is when my ears perked up. "Have to" (along with its close friends "always" and "never") is a sure sign that you're telling yourself a story. She already had a huge story in her head about what would happen if she invited X but didn't invite Y.

So, we got curious. She knows that there's not really an algorithm to decide, but was in the space of wanting to bypass the difficult feelings. When we dug into the "have to" she shared the stories that she was telling herself. They all centered around not wanting to hurt anyone's feelings. Now this is a beautiful, kind thought process. It's based in love but can be a path that leads to resentment if it's not kept in balance.

You see, her feelings were not even on her radar. Everything we dug into was about the other person.

I asked her, "If there was no possibility of anyone else's feelings being hurt, who would you want to invite?" She got pretty emotional when she answered. The truth-truth-truth often has that effect.

We dug a bit more into the difficult feelings that were underneath her desire for a decision-making-algorithm and made a plan. It's not going to be easy for her to have uncomfortable conversations. Relationships change and people are complicated, but at the end of the day,
standing in her own integrity is where joy starts. Knowing that she was true to herself is the grounding force she needed to connect to joy.

I invited her to be compassionate to herself when she wants to bypass the discomfort; to be courageous enough to have the hard conversations and to celebrate herself after she makes the choice to honor her feelings. Using these 3 Cs (compassion, courage, celebrate) makes the difficult choices feel a little kinder and helps reinforce a new thought process. It's not an algorithm but it will help her make the choices that connect her to joy.

Week 8: Love Your Process

What would happen if you stopped judging the way you do things? How would you feel if you accepted the things you didn't like as being part of your process? Could you believe that you're doing the best you can?

I can tell you that my answers are I feel free, peaceful and hell yeah!
My recent self-kindness journey has been centered around accepting the things that are part of my process and loving myself through them. I'm not talking about the run of the mill things, but the things that I love to hold against myself…like the fact that I still get anxious and a little nauseous before speaking gigs and big meetings. My refrain had been
"You should be over this by now." or "What's wrong with you that you still feel this way?"

Then I had a recent light bulb moment. You know, one of those times when all the things you've read/heard/taught come crashing together and you finally "get it."

My light bulb was simple. Accept the nausea as part of your process.
Ironically, I have a 4-year-old sticky note inside my medicine cabinet that says I will love myself through this process…but you know, sometimes we need to learn the same lesson several times!

Getting back to "How would you feel if you accepted the things you didn't like as being part of your process?" – my answer is free. The past few times I've had a speaking gig or a big meeting, I've approached my looming nerves very differently. Instead of feeling frustrated, I've prepared. That usually means skipping the coffee, eating something beige like a bagel or pasta and having Kombucha tea and mint on hand.

This small shift has made for an entirely different experience. Instead of expending even more energy being frustrated with myself, I felt the freedom of acceptance.

When you give yourself the gift of accepting even the messy things as a part of your process, you're rewarded with even deeper self-love. What messy parts of your process do you want to accept? I'd love to know.

Week 9: Self Love starts with Self Kindness

Self-love is important but it can often seem like a far-off destination. After all, if you're used to walking around and listening to your inner critic like it's speaking the truth, selflove can seem almost impossible.

Instead of trying to dive straight into self-love, start with self-kindness.

Maybe you don't know how to fall in love with yourself. It's totally OK!

Very few lifelong relationships start with love at first sight. They often start with kindness, and from there, love develops.

Your relationship with yourself develops the same way. When you start being kind to yourself you slowly start to fall in love with yourself. Self-kindness gestures can be as simple as taking yourself for a walk, listening to your favorite music or going to bed a little bit earlier. They can be as grand as speaking up for yourself, setting boundaries or finding a new job. Start wherever it's comfortable for you – there's no self-kindness gesture that's too small.

When self-kindness becomes a habit, you're on your way to self-love.

Over time, you'll start to fall in love with yourself. Like any other relationship, the feeling will develop slowly. You may notice that your choices are in your own best interest, what you accept from others in your life has shifted and you've started to realize that the inner critic voice isn't the truth. Start practicing self-kindness today and set a reminder to check in with yourself in a few months so you see just how far you've come!

Week 10: Speak Kindly to Yourself

One of things that makes the biggest impact in life on a daily basis, is speaking to yourself kindly.
    *Even when you make a mistake.
    *Even when you accidentally hurt someone's feelings.
    *Even when you do something you're not proud of.
    *Even when you don't get everything on your list done.
    *Even when you miss a deadline.
    *Even when you forget something.

Especially if you're a woman, you've been conditioned to apologize and to beat yourself up at every misstep, but it's possible to change that…even at all of those times.

Think about your best friend or closest relative. Remember a time when they came to you after making a mistake or feeling like they didn't get enough done. How did you respond?

Did you tell them they sucked or better try harder next time or that you value them less? I kinda doubt it. More likely, you responded with empathy. You told them you love them even though they're not perfect, and that it's OK to make mistakes.

What if you told yourself those things the next time you made a mistake or expected yourself to be perfect? It sounds kind of crazy at first. You might even be worried that you'll lose your edge if you cut yourself a break, but I promise the opposite is true.

Give it a try this week. Put some of that early January renewed energy to work on your self-talk, and start speaking kindly to yourself.

Week 11: The Most Important Step

Most of us don't realize how unkindly we treat ourselves. It's not uncommon to (quietly) call yourself an idiot or to berate yourself for making a mistake…and don't even get me started on what women say to themselves in the mirror.

Would you ever say any of those things to a friend? If you talked to a friend the way you talk to yourself, they probably wouldn't be your friend anymore. People don't respond very well to being treated poorly, yet we don't hesitate to treat ourselves that way. We think that to make ourselves change, we have to be harsh or even mean. Our inner drill sergeant comes out and starts barking orders at us. Make your bed every day, you slob. Skip dessert, fatso. Run another mile, lazy.

For a while we listen to that drill sergeant. We make the bed, skip dessert and run some extra miles. There's a temporary high and we're sure this will be the time we stick with all of these changes.

Then the crash comes. We eat cake at our friend's birthday party, miss the gym and stop caring about making the bed. We berate ourselves for falling off the wagon and the cycle repeats…again.

There is a different way.

Learn to be on the lookout for the inner drill sergeant and the unkind words. When you hear them, pause and think about what you'd say to a close friend. Ask yourself if you would say those things to someone you love. Think about how you would talk to a loved one, and use those words to speak to yourself.

When you fall off the wagon (because you will, we're all human), think about how you would forgive a friend for a silly mistake or small stumble. Think about how insignificant it would be to you if your friend didn't skip dessert. Apply the same truths to yourself.

Forgive yourself each time you stumble, and the stumbles will no longer feel like road blocks. Let yourself know that it's OK and you get to try again tomorrow.

This is the most important step you will ever take. I don't care what you want to change, if you start by being kind to yourself and treating yourself like a friend, you'll go further than ever before.

Week 12: Be Careful How You Talk to Yourself

If you stopped to listen to yourself, what would you hear? Would you hear words of encouragement? Praise? Confidence?

…or would you hear something more like this:

Idiot. Now look what you did. Everything looks terrible. What's wrong with you? Why can't you just get it right/done/fixed?

Now think about your best friend, or your spouse, or your child. How would you feel if someone was speaking to them the way you're talking to yourself?

Would you want to hug them and be their friend, or would you be more likely to punch them and run away?
The way you feel about the person talking to your loved one, is the same way you feel about your inner voice.

Next time you're walking around feeling like you want to punch your inner voice (AKA inner critic), try this instead:

1. **Notice it.** Really tune in. We spend so much of our time on the go, running from place to place, that we're often oblivious to the negative things we say to ourselves. Awareness is the key.
2. **Talk to it the way you would want someone to talk to your loved one.** Make a mistake at work and call yourself an idiot? Once you've noticed that, you can try again. What would you tell your best friend, spouse or child if they made a mistake? Tell that to yourself, too.
3. **Drop** the judgment. These are long-standing patterns, and change takes time. When you notice the inner critic voice, don't judge yourself for its negativity. Simply forgive yourself and remember that you're on the road to talking to yourself more kindly.

Practice these easy steps, and over time, you'll notice your relationship with yourself being way more Hug and much less Punch!

SECTION 2: The Courage to be Imperfect

www.KindOverMatter.com

Week 13: Confessions from a Recovering Perfectionist

A friend of my husband came to our house unexpectedly over the weekend. I was spending the day with my 2 closest girlfriends, so I couldn't do a last-minute-crazy-cleanup-spree.

Years ago, this would have infuriated me, and in fact it did. When the same situation happened 5 or so years ago, I was MAD! Mad because I knew my husband wouldn't do a crazy-clean-up-spree. Mad because my house wasn't "guest ready." Mad because someone might see that things aren't perfect.

I'm sure you can figure out that no one cared what my home looked like…no one except for me.

Thinking that I had to be perfect was a miserable way to live. When I think of the time and emotional energy I wasted, it's exhausting.

So why did I care so much if no one else did? My friend Jo Casey talks about feminine conditioning (our culture's rules & expectations for women) and that was definitely a part of it. Another part was the rules & expectations I had for myself.

Somewhere along the way, I'd constructed a story that the love I received from others was conditional. That if my imperfections were evident, their love would disappear. So I did my darnedest to protect myself.

The process of learning to unravel that story I'd constructed was a slow one, and the old story still pops up from time to time. It popped up over the weekend when my first reaction to not being able to do a crazy-clean-up-spree was a little flutter of anger.
The difference now is that I recognize that as an old story, not a true story.

I know that the love of the people who matter most isn't conditional…and most importantly, the love I have for myself is no longer conditional either.

Week 14: Honor the Space Between

A long time ago, I gave advice to a colleague who was struggling after missing an important deadline. He was completely stuck and paralyzed. He was in hot water and knew that he could never complete the project. It was already late and he didn't know what to do. My advice was: send what you have. Something is better than nothing.

That phrase, something is better than nothing, has stuck with me. Also, that coworker and friend from 15 years ago is now my husband, who like me, can be paralyzed by perfection.

For the most part, we are no longer paralyzed by our perfectionist ways; however, I'd be lying if I told you we were completely free of them. We are in the space between. Not yet, are we fully handling everything with ease, but no longer are we procrastinating, freezing up or numbing. We are in the space between. We have embraced "something is better than nothing" and acknowledge that mistakes happen, and progress isn't linear.

Perfection, quite simply, leads to inaction. We know we can never make our art, or home or book perfect, so we don't even try. We become obsessed with the smallest details (anyone else ever spend hours on PowerPoint fonts & shading???), and miss deadlines or stop altogether.

Friends, there is so much space in between to honor. To take a baby step toward a goal; to risk making a mistake; to accomplish something instead of nothing. These are all in between. Not a single one of us will ever be perfect. Nor will our projects, our clients, our work or our homes. Instead of punishing ourselves by giving up, let's examine the space between and acknowledge the freedom that lives there.

Week 15: Life Does Not Have to be Perfect

Dear Perfectionists,
this one's for you.

Wonderful is what we want and trying to be perfect is the only way we know how to get it. We set our bar impossibly high thinking that once we hit that goal, get that thing, reach that weight or have that success, life will be wonderful. Then we actually do hit that goal, get that thing, reach that weight and have that success, and are still left wondering when the wonderful comes. When do we get to feel wonderful? Clearly our bar wasn't set high enough, so we raise it, and the cycle begins again.

Oh cycle of striving, how familiar I am with you. You gave me some great things – lots of nice shoes & bags and the ability to buy and re-buy a wardrobe to keep up with my ever-changing body – but you never gave me wonderful. No matter how high I raised my bar, I was never able to hold on to that elusive feeling. I got glimpses of it and thought I'd finally found it; things were finally perfect, but it never stuck around.

I'll be turning 38 in a few months and have been settling into wonderful for only a couple of years. On the outside, my life looks mostly the same. I didn't lock myself in an ashram for 2 years, I swear!

What I did do was stop. I stopped the constant need to be doing, going, striving, criticizing, judging, deflecting…

I stopped the external focus.

I also started. I started listening, practicing stillness, saying no, slowing down, speaking my truth, practicing kindness…

I started looking inside.

Looking inside scared the shit out of me. What if there's nothing there that's valuable or worthy or lovable? At the end of the day, that's the biggest fear, right? What if we let our most authentic selves be visible and become unlovable? What if the mask is the only thing people love about us?

That's what kept me in the cycle of striving for years. I thought that if I could achieve some BS idea of perfect, then I'd love me. Turns out, the opposite is true. Perfection is fatally uninteresting and completely unachievable, so I was actually blocking my ability to love myself by striving for perfect.

Wonderful came when I started to love imperfection. It was scary, and at times still is, but even when it's scary, it's still wonderful.

Wonderful is real and messy and challenging and alive. It's a sense that no matter what happens, I'm OK. I've got this. It's acknowledging that life is never going to be perfect for anyone, and really knowing that perfect is an illusion.

Wonderful is the stability and calm that comes from inside, even when things are messy.

…and all of those people who I feared only loved me for the mask? Turns out they love me even more in all of my perfect imperfection.

Week 16: Make Time for Yourself

Raise your hand if you put other people's needs in front of your own.

………………I see you out there ……………………..

It's OK. Most of us do; in fact we're conditioned to do that. We're socialized to think that making time for ourselves is selfish or narcissistic.

{look at her, always putting herself first}

No one wants to be that "her".

Or do we?

She sure seems less stressed than I do. She even seems happy. Wow. I wonder what that's about.

What if it wasn't selfish to make time for yourself? What if making time for yourself actually helped you better take care of others?

I know that when I feel overwhelmed and stressed out, I tend to add things to my "to do" list, instead of subtract. It makes no sense, but I know that's my pattern. I can get so stuck in that pattern of go-go-go, that I fall back into old perfectionist habits and create completely unreasonable lists that, quite honestly, make me feel worse about myself.

In those moments, if I can be present for just a brief second, what I know is that adding crazy things to my "to do" list is a sign that I need to make time for myself. I need to step away and read a magazine, go for a walk, call a friend…anything other than adding to that list.

I'm lucky to be in a place where I understand my triggers and my habits, but it took some time. I can't promise that the presence and awareness comes overnight, but I can promise you that it does come, and making time for yourself is a big first step.

Week 17: Your Worth is Not Dependent on How Much You Do (holiday edition)

Holidays can amplify to our "busy-ness" obsessed culture. Not only do we hustle for our worthiness at work, now we've got holiday hustle added in as well.

When the holidays approach, we start stressing out about how many houses to visit, what to bring, who to buy presents for, when to wrap, what to cook, etc., etc., etc.

The list can be endless and we end up becoming whirling dervishes from mid-November until mid-January.

This time of year is the perfect amplifier to our "busy-ness" obsessed culture. Not only do we hustle for our worthiness at work, now we've got 2 months of hustle at home as well.

Unless you don't.

I'm not advocating a holiday boycott. We don't do gigantic shifts around here – but I've got some things that you might need to hear so that maybe (just, maybe!) you can actually enjoy your holidays this year, instead of being an exhausted, cranky, disconnected person.

1. You are still a good parent even if your kids' presents aren't perfectly wrapped.
2. You are still a good host even if you use paper napkins or serve pre-made food.
3. You are still a good family member even if you can't see everyone in person.
4. You are still a good friend even if you show up to someone's home empty-handed.

OK, now that we've cleared that up, let's talk turkey (which is ironic since I don't eat turkey!).

Most of us (and I'm raising my hand here) think that we have to prove something, in order to be worthy. It's an epidemic and it's making us miserable. It's reinforced in the majority of companies in America, in every advertisement and in most of society. Add in the holidays and we end up missing out on the time of year when we could be making beautiful memories with family and friends.

I invite you to approach this holiday season differently.
Consider these 2 questions:

1. What is the most important part of the holiday season to you?
2. How do you want to feel during your holiday celebrations?

Keep those 2 questions in mind as you make your way through the holidays this year. Let them be your guidepost and consult them before you over-commit, over-schedule and disconnect. Make the memories you want to make because the people who matter already know you're worthy.

Week 18: How to Take the First Step

They say that when you're trying to (re)establish an exercise habit, the hardest thing is getting out the door. After all, once you're out of the house dressed in workout gear, you're probably going to go to the gym. It's the getting out, that first step, that is so difficult.

The same is true for other changes you might want to implement. When you want to start speaking more kindly to yourself, the first step of noticing the critical voice is often the one we struggle with most.

When you want to start going to the gym it's an external habit; so you can put systems in place to support yourself. You can lay out your clothes the night before, put your gym bag by the front door or set your alarm to get up 30 minutes earlier.

Trying to speak more kindly to yourself is an internal habit, so the support system looks different – but it does exist, and it looks a little something like this:

First: Start by cultivating awareness.
We cannot change what we do not acknowledge. To begin to tune into that critical inner voice that we all have, check out what goes through your mind when you make a mistake or feel frustrated. This voice is probably speaking more than you realize and once you learn what it says. you can tune into it more often.
Second: Use compassion.
If hating ourselves created change, we'd all be perfect by now! When you notice that critical voice, greet it with compassion. Instead of being frustrated that it exists or trying to bully it into submission, give it some love. Have compassion for it – that voice is trying to keep you safe, and though its methods are questionable, it's motivation is safety.
Third: Step into courage.
Even when you want to do something differently, there's comfort in staying the same. Get courageous and tell yourself something different. If you notice that your inner voice tells you that your project will never impress the client, courageously step into the possibility that it will. Consider the possibility that the client will love your work. Consider

the possibility that they'll be super impressed and you'll have done a great job. No fake mantras here, just the courageous choice to consider that something good is possible.

Fourth: CELEBRATE!

Celebrate the courageous step you took, no matter what the outcome. You just did the thing! You noticed your inner critical voice, treated it with compassion and courageously stepped into a different way of speaking to yourself. CELEBRATE YOURSELF! Give yourself the credit you deserve for making this change. The more you celebrate yourself, the more likely you are to stick with your new system.

Want a quick way to remember this? Think of the 3 Cs: compassion, courage, celebrate. Once you've got the awareness around the internal dialog you'd like to shift, using the 3Cs will create the framework to help you make that change.

Week 19: You Deserve the Support You Give

"Who is your 'you'?" I asked her. She had just finished telling me that she loves supporting those closest to her and helping them solve problems, yet she described sharing her own challenges as being a burden to others.

When I asked who she went to for support, the answer was a quiet, "no one." Probing a bit more, we discovered that she judged herself very differently than those she loved. When they came to her for support she never considered them weak or felt they were a burden; yet that's exactly how she described herself for needing support. It was absolutely OK for them but she shouldn't need it.

Are you walking around with the same double standard and not letting yourself be supported?

Dig into that a bit. Think about the people you love most, and for whom you provide support. Imagine a close friend or family member calling you to talk about a challenging situation. What's your first thought? Is it a judgment about their weakness or anger at them for burdening you?

I bet it's not. More likely you feel a deep sense of caring for them. You might even feel honored that they trust you enough to be vulnerable. You're a part of their inner circle and have earned their trust.

Consider for a moment that they could feel the same about you. Imagine that their first thought when you seek support isn't that you're a burden but that they feel honored that you trust them enough to reach out.
I'm betting that the people you love are close to you for a reason…and I bet if you give them a chance, they'll show you just how much they want to support you the next time you're knocked down.

Week 20: Learn to Believe the Good Thoughts

Thoughts aren't facts. Wait. What? They're not the be all, end all, truthiest of truths?

Nope. Sorry, love. I may be bursting your bubble, but it's important that you know that not every thought you have is true.

So how do you know which ones to believe? We're getting to that. First, we need to start by acknowledging that you get to choose which thoughts to believe. I know, this is getting a little "woo woo," but stay with me. Science is coming!

Maybe this feels familiar: You're bopping along in the morning, feeling pretty good. It's a good hair day, you got enough sleep and the coffee was strong. Then, you catch a sideways glance in the mirror and think, "These pants make me look awful." You know what happens next. The whole feel good morning is out the window. You spend the next 20
minutes digging through your closet trying on everything in there, but at this point you already know everything looks awful, so the foul mood continues.

How does that happen? How do we go from feeling good to a being in a foul mood with 1 fleeting negative thought? Science says it's because our brains have a negativity bias. We're up to 5 times more likely to remember bad things than good things, and the same applies to
our thoughts.

Translation: It takes work to cultivate a pattern of believing the good things and thoughts.

Here's how to do it:

First, you've got to tune in. Start to pay attention to what you think and how you feel. For me, I know I'm stressed when my fists are clenched. That's my sign to check out my thinking and see what's going on. (It's usually not good!) **Next, once you notice the negative thought or something in your body, take a breath**. Relax your body. Unclench your fists and relax your shoulders.

Finally, remind yourself of 5 good things. I'm not talking about mantras that you don't quite buy into, but 5 real things. In the pants example above, those 5 things could be: I'm having a good hair day, my coffee was delicious, I feel really well rested, I have energy, I'm on time for work.

These are all choices. It takes practice, but as you start to tune in and remind yourself of good things, you're giving that negativity bias a run for its money and you're choosing to believe the good.

Week 21: You are More than Your Mistakes

If I asked you to tell me the last 5 awesome things you did, could you do it? Does it make you uncomfortable to think about the great things you've done?

What if I asked about your last 5 mistakes? I bet you could easily rattle off at least that many. We walk around keeping a running tally of our mistakes, missteps and flaws. If that's not enough, turn on your TV or scroll through social media and you'll be bombarded with ads to fix the things you didn't even know are wrong with you. Hair too thin or too thick? There's a product for that. Feeling like you're too thin or too fat? There's a product for that, too.

Of course, you can't easily talk about what makes you awesome! You're constantly surrounded by messages reinforcing the idea that something is wrong with you…and you've got that running tally of your mistakes to back them up.

All of these things take their toll. The running tally we keep, the zillions of products designed to fix our every flaw…they become a heavy load to carry and we start to feel that our mistakes are our identity. They become who we are, not things that have happened.

So, we buy the product that's designed to solve our problem and we feel lighter for a while, but inevitably the load becomes heavy again. This becomes the roller coaster of our life, and we never get off of it long enough to realize how much more there is.

There's so much more to you than your mistakes.
Your mistakes are not your identity. You're a beautiful, wondrous, flawed, exquisite creature just like me.

Put down that load for a few minutes and think about some successes you've had. Remind yourself of the things that make you awesome. Email them to yourself so that on those days when the load is feeling especially heavy and you're confusing your mistakes with your identity, you can read that list to yourself and remember that there's so much more to you than your mistakes.

Week 22: You're Too Important

You're too important to let anyone else be responsible for your life.

You're too important to measure your value by what you cross off a to do list.

You're too important to not take care of yourself.

I used to believe that if I wasn't hard on myself, nothing would ever change. Didn't get to the gym? Better remind yourself that you're lazy so you get there tomorrow. Didn't nail the presentation at work? Better stay later to make up for it. Didn't get the laundry done? Better berate yourself for being a terrible housekeeper so you stay up all night doing it.

I never questioned these thoughts. Somehow, I just fell into the habit of being hard on myself. After all, everyone else seemed to be doing the same thing, so that must be the way to get things done, right?

Wrong. Taking responsibility for my life taught me the opposite is true. Being hard on myself was actually a setup for failure, not success. That when I am kind to myself, I can actually make changes, and make them stick. That when I listen to what I need, I'm much happier than when I have a long list of crossed off tasks.

You're too important not to.

Week 23: Imperfect is Beautiful

For a long time, I used my imperfections against myself. I could easily ramble off a long list of them, but that's not relevant. What is relevant, is what I now know to be true. What makes us different and imperfect is what makes us beautiful.

Some of the most wonderful things in nature are imperfect. Have you ever tasted an ugly ripe tomato? I can tell you, they are FAR more delicious than their beautiful, perfectly red & round on the vine counterparts. In fact, for years, tomatoes have been grown for looks,
not taste. Huh. Well doesn't that sound familiar. Even tomatoes are judged by how they look, not their substance.

The messages are clear. You can't turn on a TV, open a magazine or browse social media without getting the message that perfect is what's expected. Every product advertisement is trying to fix whatever imperfections you have. Skin too oily? There's a product to make it
perfect. Skin too dry? That's not perfect either, so here's a product for that.

Look, I love makeup and beauty products and hair color a lot, and in no way am I advocating against them. What I care about is the motivation behind them. I color my hair because I love bright red hair. I use makeup because I choose to enhance certain features.

It's when we get caught up in the eternal striving for perfection, that we risk becoming those round, bright red tomatoes…that have very little taste. Ugly ripe tomatoes had to fight for their place in stores, but they got it. Substance won. Imperfect won. Their beauty is so much more than what's on the surface. They are odd and imperfect and beautiful, and I love them…just like me.

SECTION 3: Kind Living

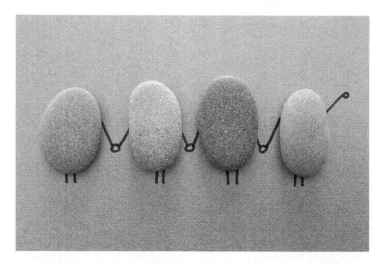

www.KindOverMatter.com

Week 24: What Lights You Up?

She had recently heard about the 4-burner theory on life: work, family, friends, health… and quickly revealed that her work burner was boiling over, and had been for years. Family & friends got squeezed in, and were understanding of her demanding career, but health was sorely neglected.

She also knew that wasn't a maintainable way to live. As a leader in her organization, her mental and physical health are the heart of her success, yet they're the lowest items on her priority list.

I hear this story so often – successful, driven, professional women who are on the verge of burnout and ready to make a shift. There's fear there (*Can I still be successful? YES – probably even more so!*); but more than fear, there's a glimmer of hope…a tiny spark of belief that things can feel better. That spark is the light that carries you forward. It gradually grows brighter as you take baby steps toward a different kind of life. After a few months, it's bright enough to illuminate the new path…and that's when most of us think our work is done. The truth is that's where it begins again.

Once you hit the place of knowing the new choices you want to make, the work shifts. At that point, it becomes about maintaining. What do you do when you hit a bump in the road? What do you do when your progress goes in the wrong direction?

Come back to what lights you up.

If you're reading this and remembering that magic time when things seemed shiny and bright but are feeling very differently right now, think about what got you to the shiny, bright place. What choices did you make? Did you sleep more or eat differently? Were you reading at night instead of watching TV? Was there more connection with family and friends?

Start small (always start small!) and follow the light. Reconnect to that little spark as often as needed. Keep coming back to the things that light you up.

Week 25: Be a Kindness Hero

When Americans celebrate Independence Day, we start to hear a lot about heroes. We think of those who fought for freedom and to make a better world. Those people are capital H Heroes for sure.

There are also heroes who make the world a better place in a different way. Maybe it's by volunteering time, helping those less fortunate, advocating for animals, donating money or being politically involved. All of those people are heroes, as well.

You know who else is a hero?

Anyone who shows kindness to a stranger.

Anyone who doesn't yell back at the person who flips them off in traffic.

Anyone who kindly questions the intentions of a cranky colleague instead of talking about them behind their back.
Anyone who takes the time to compliment someone for a job well done.

Anyone who cares for themselves and practices self-kindness.

Heroes make the world a better place and there are endless ways to do that. As we honor the capital H Heroes, let's also honor ourselves for being kindness heroes. You're making the world a better place and that's the best definition of being a hero there is.

Week 26: Kindness is Always Fashionable

When I was in the 5th grade, I was awarded the Lions Club Citizenship award for Kindness. I was probably wearing leg warmers when I accepted the medal, and I know I had a home perm…hello child of the 1980s!

Thankfully I'm no longer wearing leg warmers, and it's safe to say that my home perm days are behind me. What remains, though, is kindness. No matter what stage in my life, what fashion trend I'm observing or what I'm doing with my hair, kindness is there.

Kindness is a value I hold and it informs how I show up in the world. It's always been important to me to treat others kindly, even though it took me until my 30s to extend that same consistent kindness to myself.

What's so clear to me now, is the incredibly strong relationship between the two. The kinder I am to myself, the more kindness I'm able to extend to others. When I'm being critical of myself, I'm more critical of others. When I'm running myself ragged and not taking care of my body and mind, I'm less likely to give others the grace they deserve.

When I'm holding things against myself, I'm less able to forgive others' small slips.

Consider your own value of kindness. How do you practice it? How is it impacted by the way you're treating yourself? When you learn to recognize the relationship between kindness to others and self-kindness, you gain a whole new level of understanding, so the next time you notice yourself being unusually critical of others, take a look at how you're treating yourself.

Week 27: A Different Kind of Valentine's Love

When Valentine's day comes around, you might get just as sick of the jewelry, chocolate and greeting card commercials as I do. I love love, and am all for celebrating love, but we're going to do that a little differently today. No trip up the greeting card aisle, no gift to buy.

Today, I want you to celebrate the ways you love yourself.

Not sure where to start? Let's start by celebrating your uniqueness! You are the only you who will ever walk the planet, forever and ever and ever, yet most of us go around wishing we were more like "everyone else"…especially when you're bombarded with ads for products that tell you there's something wrong with you.

So, just for today, I invite you to notice your uniqueness and celebrate it. Whenever you start to hear the voice of comparison (which, by the way, is one of the most common ways we fall out of love with ourselves) remind yourself of 1 way your uniqueness makes you awesome.

Try this simple celebration of self-love today: notice comparison, identify 1 way you're unique and tell yourself why that uniqueness makes you awesome.

Repeat as needed!

Week 28: Set Intentions, Not Resolutions

*First, you certainly don't need to wait until a new year to make a change. Sure it's easy to get carried away with all that "new year, new you" momentum, but that's also a great way to avoid taking action the other 364 days of the year.

*Second, resolutions rarely include a plan and almost never include support. These 2 things are KEY to making changes last.

*Third, they often end up as something we hold against ourselves for 11 months out of the year. If you've ever been to a gym in January versus June, you can understand what I'm saying!

So, what do you do instead? How do you honor the energy of this time without setting yourself up for failure with another mile-long list of resolutions?

Set intentions, not resolutions.

Intentions are an energetic invitation. They're a declaration to the universe that you're ready to receive something new. They're a touchstone that you can use as a guide, and come back to throughout the year. They're not a list of things that, if not accomplished, diminish your sense of self-worth and value.

Here's how they work:

* Did you resolve to go to the gym 3 times per week? Change that to an intention of valuing health and movement.
*Did you resolve to quit smoking? Change that to an intention of learning better stress management.
*Did you resolve to start a meditation practice? Change that to an intention of living mindfully.

See the difference? Resolutions are limiting, and much less likely to be maintainable. Intentions are more expansive. They allow us to honor the desires at the root of the resolution in a realistic, maintainable way.

Week 29: 3 Ways to (kindly) Leave Awkward Holiday (or any!) Conversations

From holiday parties to summer BBQs, there are particular times of year when we see people we haven't seen all year, attend parties with folks we don't know very well, and visit with family and extended family.

Between sips of eggnog or lemonade, there will be lots of catching up and potentially some awkward conversations. You know the ones – where your 3rd cousin twice removed starts probing for some family gossip, or the partner of a colleague in another department starts trying to dig for juicy office information. There are always going to be people who want to tell other peoples' stories, but you don't have to join in.

When you find yourself stuck in one of those not-so-happy-party-times, here are some ways to extract yourself, kindly, so you can get back to the cheer!

This one's for you **if this entire concept makes you feel REALLY uncomfortable**, but you know you want to stop participating in the gossip scene: I need some more eggnog/punch/tea/vodka. Shall I get you some, too? –This gives you the perfect reason to walk away and leave the conversation. If you need to return to that person, use the break to change the subject.

This one's for **you if you're comfortable enough to permanently exit the conversation**: I just remembered that I need to find Suzie, Joe, Sally, etc., before they leave, please excuse me. –This one helps you physically exit the space.

This one's for you **if you're feeling like a rock-star with boundaries**: It's great to see you, and I'd love to hear more about you. I'm not comfortable discussing someone else's situation, so tell me about your plans for New Year's Eve! –This one redirects the conversation while kindly letting the other person know your feelings on gossip.

Whatever level you're at, remember that you have a choice. You don't need to endure the party gossip circuit. Use these ideas to create spaces that feel how you want them to feel, and maximize your party enjoyment!

Week 30: Always Be a Little Kinder than Necessary

I've been struggling a little with being kind this week.

Yuck. That feel gross to admit, but it's true. I got pretty snappy with a hospital orderly who went past a family member's room twice without taking the dinner tray, finding a daily kindness this week has been quite a challenge, and I've just generally not felt like it.

Kinda weird to write about being kinder then, right?
Well, I figured I needed a reminder of how I want to show up, and more importantly, some gentleness around my own human imperfection.

Yes, I always want to be a little kinder than necessary. That's how I want to show up in the world whether it's with a client, my husband or a perfect stranger. There's so much negativity and terribleness in the world, I really feel drawn to sharing some light. That's my goal, but the reality is that I don't always achieve that goal…and that's OK.

I'm not perfect (duh!) and in times like these when I'm struggling with being a little kinder than necessary, what becomes so important is self-kindness. Letting myself off the hook, knowing that I'll try again tomorrow and forgiving myself. All of those things that don't necessarily come naturally, but are so important to practice.

I spent some time this past weekend doing just that. Reflecting, pausing and letting go. It's OK that I wasn't the greatest at my kindness goal last week because I choose to keep trying. I choose to practice gentleness with myself because I know I'm going to try again.
So, here's me. Trying again. Practicing. Because life is a one-time offer, and I choose love.

Week 31: Conversations Connect Us

When I was a teenager, I would be on the phone until all hours of the night (and early morning!) having those dramatic teenage conversations. As much as I look back at them and sometimes cringe, I also have a sense of whimsy about them. For as much as they were filled with teen drama, to the best of my adolescent ability, they were real and they connected me to my closest friends.

Today, there are endless ways to have a conversation. You can text, Facebook message, Tweet, Snap or email. When was the last time you used the phone app on your pocket computer and heard someone's voice? When was the last time you had a real conversation? I'm not talking about exchanging pleasantries with coworkers or commenting on the weather. I'm talking about the kind of conversation that feels like an adventure…the kind that fills your soul and makes you think.

Conversations connect us and human beings are hard wired for connection. We also deeply fear being alone, which can explain our reluctance to having those thought provoking, vulnerable conversations. What if the other person disagrees? That's risky territory. Not everyone in your life has earned the right to those conversations, but if you're lucky, you've got a select few who have.

So, grab your pocket computer and pull up the telephone app. Call one of the folks who has earned the right to have a real, vulnerable, adventurous conversation with you. Invite that person to coffee, tea, wine or a meal. Start an adventure. Have a conversation and remember how good it feels to connect.

Week 32: Kindness is a Lifestyle

I learned a lot of lessons in 2014 when I did my #365daysofkind project. One of the biggies, is that kindness is a lifestyle.

Somehow we've ended up in a world where things that I consider common courtesy, are often surprising to people. Simple acts such as holding a door, giving a seat to someone who needs it or having pleasant conversation with a cashier, are more infrequent than I
ever realized.

The kindness lifestyle has stayed with me, and as the years go by, it's more important than ever.

We can't change the fact that kindness isn't as common as it once was. We can't prevent bad things from happening. What we can do is live a lifestyle of kindness. We can be the person who smiles at strangers. We can be the one who gives up a seat for someone who is struggling. We can choose to trust that the grumpy cashier is doing the best she can.

Living a life of kindness to ourselves and others, is a powerful choice. It sets an example for everyone we encounter. Your smile may be the only one someone gets that day. Holding a door may lighten someone's load. Saying hello could brighten the day of a stranger.

These simple choices are so much bigger than we realize. They are changing the world.

Week 33: Change the World with Kindness

In the spirit of #365DaysofKind (which is the project I did in 2014 where I did – you guessed it - an act of kindness every day for a year!), today we're talking about Random Acts of Kindness, or #RAoK, and how they truly can change the world.

While I don't think I've changed the whole world, I do know that I've made an impact. Every kind act makes an impact, and here is the story of some of my favorite impacts.

Ironically, the acts of kindness that got the most Facebook attention were ones done while I was travelling to New Orleans in March! We ended up meeting a woman from Philadelphia, living on the streets with her dog, so we all kindly gave her some money.

Another Facebook favorite was the time I waited to hold a door for someone juggling packages, who told me not to wait. I simply did what I hoped someone would do for me, but all of the wonderful KOM-ers, really identified with that one.

My personal favorite was the day I was in the city for lunch, in a monsoon! I tend to be a little dramatic, but, seriously, it was a monsoon. I was running back to my car, wearing a raincoat and carrying a huge umbrella, when I passed a woman wearing a dress, with no
umbrella or raincoat. I gave her my umbrella, and continued running to my car. This one made my heart smile SO much because it truly was the most random. I wouldn't recognize this woman again if I tripped over her, but in that moment, she was so grateful.

I've gotten some flak for publicizing my daily acts of kindness, but why shouldn't we be proud of the kind things we do for the world? I do other kind things that are private, but I love sharing my #365daysofkind journey with all of you, and reading about your kind acts!

A KOM-er commented that she bought a bouquet of flowers and gave them out to strangers on the street. I LOVE that #RAoK (and may totally copy it!), so why not inspire each other? Why not motivate each other to do good?

In a world filled with constant news reports of terrible things, I agree with the #RAoK movement.

Maybe I did change the world. My world.

SECTION 4: Life Lessons

www.KindOverMatter.com

Week 34: 3 Steps to Help You Learn from Hurt

You might not want to hear this but there's usually a lesson in the things that hurt us. I say usually because as much as I believe many things happen for a reason, I also believe that some things just suck.

For now, let's look at the "usuallys," and let's also look at something that's in the past. If there's one thing I know at my core to be true it's that we need to process hurts as they happen, and save the lessons for the future.

So start by calling a past event to mind that in the moment, felt hurtful. Maybe it was a challenge with a coworker, maybe you felt like you let someone down, or maybe someone spoke to you unkindly.

Got your situation ready? Great!

Here's a simple way to start to see the lesson that life might be trying to teach you:
1. Visualize the hurtful event as specifically as possible. What were you wearing? Where were you? Who was there? Try to clearly see yourself in that past situation.

2. Once you've got your event visualized, remember what you said and did and how you acted. Take a breath or two here and give yourself a moment of self-kindness.

3. Ask your present-self two questions: Is this feeling familiar? How would I handle this situation today?

The first question (Is this familiar?) will help you notice if the hurtful situation is a pattern in your life. Maybe you gravitate toward folks who don't always treat you with kindness. Maybe you see a pattern in feeling that you let people down. Maybe the challenge with the coworker feels eerily similar to a childhood situation. Whatever you discover is key to the lesson. We don't tend to see our own patterns unless we specifically look for them. Patterns are a big neon sign pointing you toward a lesson you can learn.

The second question (How would I handle this situation today?) lets you approach the hurtful scenario from a calm place. When you're in the moment it's difficult to make a calm decision, but once you examine something that's already happened you can choose actions carefully. Practice this one a few times, especially if you identified a pattern when you asked yourself the first question. The more you practice your desired response when you're calm, the more likely you'll be able to make small changes, and react differently in the future.

Play with these 3 steps and get curious – particularly if you identified a pattern. Let your calm present self be your teacher and use the lessons underneath your past hurts to help shape your future.

Week 35: Ask for What You Need

I've been having a lot of conversations around boundaries and using your voice lately which tells me it's something I need to pay attention to in my own life. Ever notice that?

When something appears in multiple other places or with multiple other people in your realm, there's usually something there for you, too. That's definitely the case for me. So, I started paying attention…and I learned (re-learned?) some important lessons.

It's hard to ask for what you need. There are about a gazillion reasons why asking for what you need is a challenge. From girls being socialized to be sweet, quiet and agreeable to wanting to appear like you have it all together and don't ever need to ask for help from anyone.

Boundaries are the short-term discomfort that prevent long-term tension. Boundaries are a big part of self-kindness in my world, and this is why. When we don't set them, or we don't enforce them, we're avoiding some short-term discomfort and creating long-term tension.

The story about what might happen if you ask for what you need or set a boundary is ALWAYS worse than what happens when you do either of those things. Truth. That screaming match or door slamming you imagined or feared is pretty unlikely to actually happen. Yes, these can be uncomfortable conversations, but I've yet to have one (or hear of anyone having one) that's nearly as bad as what they feared.

We all need some help with this stuff. Everyone needs a reminder sometimes, and everyone needs support when they're trying to change old habits. After all, there can be discomfort with change. Engage your support system. Whether it's one of your best friends, a coach or therapist or all of the above, getting support helps you do the hard stuff and keeps you on track.

I noticed all of these things when I tuned in to my own life and I'm so glad I did. Walking my talk is how I practice integrity, and right now that looks like doing my own next level work.

Week 36: Just Do the Next Right Thing

I love to dream big. I know that it's the details that trip me up, that I don't like "busy work," and that I need to take action when I feel inspired. It's fun to talk about the big things! The huge goals, the giant plans and heck, in January people are always talking about all of their resolutions…and a few weeks after that many of those people will be wondering why they didn't stick with those resolutions.

As a dreamer, strategizer and big-picture-seer, I know how easy it is to let the details be the downfall of an idea. When it comes to taking action it's often so overwhelming to figure out how to get from A to Z that we forget about B through Y.

Just do the next right thing.

Seriously. No matter what your goal or plan is, remembering these 6 words is key. Maybe you're like me and you can see the destination. You know what you want to change or build and you can see it clear as day…OR maybe right now you're feeling a little stuck and don't know how to get out of your current rut.

Whatever your current situation, just look for the next right thing.

That's it. Then repeat. Words to live by, how to avoid overwhelm, the key to making change…all rolled into 1 simple (but not always easy) phrase: just do the next right thing.

Week 37: Small Changes are the Foundation of Growth

"I'm pretty proud of how I'm handling things, even though everything is up in the air right now."

It was true. She was navigating some professional changes, dealing with a new health challenge and her partner was in job transition. When it comes to the big parts of life, everything really was in flux.

When we met, she was (admittedly) in desperate need of self-care. She had a paralyzing fear of saying no to anyone, and as a result was feeling stressed, anxious and resentful.

That was over a year ago, and we started slowly. She knew she wanted to set boundaries, but saying no felt impossible. So, we took the pressure off and I told her she didn't have to say no. Instead, she could simply Pause: In the moments when people are asking something of you, simply tell them you'll get back to them tomorrow. By giving herself the space to breathe before responding to a request, she was able to start responding from a calmer place, and saying no was suddenly possible. Starting small helped her learn that small changes are the foundation of growth.

She's had a year to really hone her boundary-setting skills and has come so far. She created a fulfilling life for herself and her schedule was no longer filled with obligatory things that she didn't want to do. She had more time for the important relationships in her life (and was actually enjoying them again), and she was practicing self-care by reconnecting to some long-lost hobbies.

And then a few months ago, things started hitting the fan.

When I talk about building a solid self-kindness foundation (which includes setting boundaries and kindly saying no), this is why. Life throws us curve balls. If the stressed, anxious and resentful woman I originally met had been thrown into her current situation, things would have gone a lot differently. Because she's built a strong foundation, she's able to handle the challenges that life has recently thrown at her…and I'm pretty proud of how she's handling things, too.

Week 38: Helping Others Helps You

I love doing kind things for other people. Whether it's making a surprise breakfast for my husband or helping a stranger struggling with bags at the grocery store, I love seeing their reaction. It feels good to make people happy.

Did you know that doing kind things for others, is one of the kindest things you can do for yourself? Turns out there are scientific reasons it feels so good to do kind things for others!

Among other benefits, doing kind things for others leads to improved cognitive performance, an increase in energy and lower heart rate. Yup. Being kind can actually make you healthier, and being healthier definitely makes you feel happier.

So find some ways you can do kind things for others this week, and see how much better you feel!

Week 39: Walk Your Talk

There have been many times in my life when I've felt stuck, and that's one of the biggest reasons people come to me for coaching. They can't see a way out of a bind, they've hit a wall or they're at a crossroads.

Good ole stuckness. It can be a tough one to get out of, and everybody wants to find the perfect process or to-do list to get themselves unstuck. If only it were that simple…

You're completely capable of making a list, creating a strategy or setting up a step-by-step plan to get unstuck. You've probably done it a million times, and even had some success, albeit fleeting. There's something more.

I talk a lot about self-kindness, and firmly believe in the power of being kind to yourself. I'm also far from perfect, so there are plenty of days when I'm criticizing myself for something I did, something I said, or how I look. When I have too many of those days in a row, I get stuck, and no to-do list can get me unstuck.

When I'm not walking my talk, stuckness sets in. How can I talk to people about doing something I'm not doing myself? It simply doesn't work. As soon as I start walking my talk again, things open up. The stuckness dissipates and life falls back into place.

Loving myself first is the key. I have to make the choice to love myself enough to really look at where I'm not walking my talk, and make a different choice. Maybe you're a teacher, who doesn't want to learn. Maybe you're a nurse who can't let anyone take care of you. Maybe you're a manager trying to instill confidence in your team, but you still find yourself jumping at every email from a leader.

However you're stuckness is showing up, love yourself enough to look at it through a new lens. Stop trying to fix it with a system, a process, research or a to-do list, and start looking at where you're not walking your talk. It'll all start to fall into place.

Week 40: Change Your Words, Change Your Life

How do you talk to yourself?

Most people have no idea how to answer this question. Except for the occasional times when the voice in the back of your head gets really loud, you generally just ignore it. You have a constant chatter going on in the back of your mind, but never really stop to listen to it.

What if you did? What would it say? Is that voice encouraging, telling you to go for it; or is it holding you back and telling you you can't do something? Mine tends to be a mix of both, depending on the situation.

When you start tuning into that voice in the background, you can change it. You can choose to speak kindly to yourself and build a strong foundation.

The words you speak really do become the house you live in. Your words = your house. Do you want to live in a house built on a foundation of kindness? Start listening to that voice.

Join me this week in tuning into that voice. When it's discouraging or scared, try to show it some love and kindness – let it know that you've got this. Let's build our foundation of self-kindness together.

Week 41: We Are Our Choices

I read a quote recently that said you can blame your parents until you're 30, but after that, it's time to take responsibility. OK, truthfully it said you can bitch about your parents until you're 30; after that, shut up! LOL

Clearly it made me laugh, but it also made me think…and I think taking responsibility is sexy. Yes, we've all been shaped by things that happened in our past. By no means am I discounting that. I'm saying that it doesn't have to be an either/or situation. It can be an AND.

Maybe things were pretty crappy when you were a kid. Some of the most inspirational people came from some pretty scary circumstances. The choices they made as adults are what made the difference. Every single day you wake up, you have a choice…AND you can choose to learn a different way.

Maybe your childhood was idyllic, but adulthood hasn't been all that happy. You have the power to make a different choice. What's one way you can choose happiness?

As sexy as it is to take responsibility, it's also hard work. Our ingrained habits and patterns of thinking can absolutely be changed, but it's not instant gratification. One choice after the other, change happens.

Growth happens. You take your power back, all starting with a choice.

Your choices speak volumes. What do you want yours to say?

Week 42: May Your Choices Reflect Your Hopes

For small words, hope and fear are a pretty big deal. They are powerful forces.

Hope has been the symbol of everything from presidential campaigns to cancer research organizations. It's everywhere, and gets a lot of good press.

Fear, on the other hand, is the bad guy. We are taught to hate fear, to squash fear and to eliminate fear, but do we even really understand how fear shows up?

For many years, my choices were a reflection of fear. My choices were largely centered around appearing to have it all together. There was no connection to my feelings and my biggest fear was being 'found out'. What if everyone knew my shit was messy? What if all these feelings start leaking out? What if I'm not in control? *Outing my HUGE-est fear there, friends!*

At the time, I had no idea that I was being driven by fear, but in looking back, it's so clear to me. All of my choices came down to that 1 small-big word. Fear was in charge, and just as I wasn't connected to my fear-centered choosing, the option of hope wasn't even on my radar. Sure, I *hoped* that my relationship would get better, or that I'd find a place I wanted to live, but true hope (the kind that comes from deep in your gut) was completely unknown to me, and my choices reflected that.

I talk a lot about letting things go, and being in touch with feelings (including fear!). I believe this work heals and is the critical first step in building a strong foundation. Just as critical, though, is choice. Once you've done the feeling work, choices start to look very different.

When I started building my foundation, and wanting to feel differently, I started choosing differently. Real hope crept in and very slowly, probably not even visible to others, my choices started to reflect it.

These small steps, fueled by hope, were more powerful than fear ever was.

Week 43: The Power of a Daily Gratitude Practice

I used to roll my eyes at the idea of a gratitude journal and as someone who is old enough to remember when Oprah's show first came on the air, I had many years of eye rolling!

I still don't keep a gratitude journal but I do have a daily gratitude practice. Once I got over myself and figured out how to make this practice work for me…I was hooked.

My practice takes a few different forms and they look a little something like this:

*Every night as I'm laying in bed I come up with at least 3 things I'm grateful for that day. I bring them to mind, let them make me smile and try to make my last thoughts before sleep be good ones. (This one is a non-negotiable and has been a consistent practice for a couple of years.)

*I recently added a grateful thought in the morning. Instead of the usual wake up thought of "I'm tired, I'm cold, where's the freaking snooze button?" I consciously think about something good – maybe my comfortable bed, a warm shower or a project for the day – so that I can start my day on a positive note. (Some days I still forget to do this but I'm working on creating this habit.)

*I'm feeling stressed, overwhelmed or anxious; I connect to gratitude in the simplest way possible. I'm grateful I'm breathing, I'm grateful I'm healthy – whatever feels accessible in that moment to ground myself. (This one is an as-needed practice that comes in super handy.)

Since I've been doing these things I notice that I'm better able to stay grounded. Whether it's a stressful conversation with a loved one or a big speaking engagement, I'm operating from a more grounded place in general and my capacity to handle the curve balls of life has noticeably increased.

If you're like me and you've been rolling your eyes at the idea of a gratitude journal, or a gratitude practice in general, I get it…AND I encourage you to give it a try this week. It really is as powerful as people say.

Week 44: 3 Ways to Learn What to Ignore

One of the most powerful lessons you learn in life is learning what to ignore. From unsolicited comments to the voice of the inner critic, some things are worth paying attention to and some things are meant to be ignored. Learning that distinction, though, is easier said than done!

Here are 3 of my favorite ways to get started:

1. **Is it kind?** This is the best place to start because even criticism can be delivered kindly. Whatever the message you're hearing, whether it's from a friend, coworker or manager, only listen to the feedback that is delivered with kind words.
Don't believe criticism can be delivered kindly? Try this example. You want to communicate to someone that the work they did wasn't up to the level you expected. Unkind criticism says, "This project sucks, and I expected better from you. " Kind criticism says, "This work isn't at the same level of what you normally turn in. Did you encounter any difficulties that we can address?" That may be an extreme example but it illustrates a key difference. The unkind criticism is highly reactive and not delivered in a considerate manner. Listening to this will provide no value and in fact, will likely have a negative impact. The kind criticism opens up the opportunity to learn and offers a supportive environment. This type of criticism is not only easier to hear, but it creates the space to improve with support.

2. **Is it true?** The voice of the inner critic likes to use absolutes. "You never do this" and "You always do that" are prime examples of inner critic statements. They're also prime examples of things to ignore. When you notice your inner dialog has this absolute quality to it, take a minute and ask yourself if it's true. Is it really true that you always show up late or that you never parallel park without hitting the curb?
When you hear those absolutes it's a sure sign that what the voice is saying isn't true, and that it's something you can ignore.

3. **Is the source of the comment in my inner circle?** Feedback, comments and criticism come at us from all angles all day long. From random people in the grocery store line to colleagues who you rarely engage with, it can be a lot

to process. If you're at the point of overwhelm and can't even distinguish if what you're hearing is kind or
true, consider the source. What role does the person play in your life? Do you trust that person? If the person is a very peripheral part of your life and/or you don't trust them, feel free to disregard their comments.

The next time you encounter some feedback or comments, try passing it through these 3 questions. Notice how it's delivered and if it's kind. Ask yourself if the inner critic's comments are true. Decide if the person commenting is part of your inner circle. Start learning how to make the distinction between what's important and what's best left ignored.

Week 45: Lessons in Trust

Look at what those you trust most give to you, and start giving it to yourself.

"I don't know if I trust myself" she said to me, as we discussed a new professional opportunity that had just presented itself. You see, less than a year ago, she was a total workaholic and this new project had the potential to trigger all of those old habits. These days, she's very clear on the importance of balance in her life, time with friends and family, but the changes she's made are very new, and as they say, old habits die hard.

We explored the opportunity a bit, and got clear on the fact that she really wanted to do the work…but the lingering voice of self-doubt was screaming at the top of its lungs. *"What if I take this project and feel stuck again?"* *"What if I lose everything I've worked so hard to get back?"* *"I just don't trust myself."*

Trusting yourself is an abstract concept and it's almost impossible to describe. How do you know if you trust yourself? Not many people can articulate that feeling, so that's not where we started. Instead, we looked at the relationships with people she trusted most.

I like to call them the inner circle – the ones who have seen you at your best and at your messiest…AKA the people you'd call to bail you out!

What makes you trust the people in your inner circle? For me, it's knowing that they love all of my parts. We've had disagreements, they've seen me when I feel like I'm losing my mind and on the best days of my life, and they keep showing up. For her, it was their support, validation and fully seeing her.

Where do you give yourself the same things your inner circle gives you? That question is a little harder to answer, and it's one that I regularly come back to. My inner circle loves and accepts me completely. That's why I trust them. Hers gives her consistent support, appropriate validation and makes her feel truly seen. This is where we start when we need to (re)build trust in ourselves.

Look at what those you trust most give to you, and start giving it to yourself.

By the end of our call, we'd come up with a plan. She committed to making the choices that support building trust in herself…including taking that new professional opportunity.

Week 46: How to Feel Free

There's a kind of freedom that allows you to laugh with reckless abandon and feel love in every cell in your body. It's big and expansive and real, and it feels very different than the muted experience that is so familiar to many of us. You know the one, where every minute is perfectly scheduled and every box is checked from the house to the car to the job. The one where you're always smiling and telling people everything's fine.

I know that muted experience well, and I know how easy it is to think "that's just life." You can brush it off and tell yourself that everybody's doing it, so it must be OK.

What if you pause for a moment? What thoughts and feelings do you notice? How does it feel to stop? What happens in your body? Take a deep breath and really tune into that body of yours.

That perfectly scheduled life has a way of keeping your body constricted and your feelings pushed away. Maybe your shoulders are tense or your neck aches or your posture is continuously hunched over. Maybe you noticed some joy or sadness pop up.

Now take a moment and check in with your body again. Take a deep breath and invite in some freedom. Try straightening up your posture and rolling your neck a bit. What happens to your thoughts and feelings when you invite freedom into your body?

When you take a moment here and there to pause and to step out of that perfectly scheduled life, you're inviting in freedom. When you make this a consistent practice and find many moments to pause, you start to realize how much of life you weren't experiencing. Invite that in, too. Start to make your own practice of freedom.

Side effects of this practice may include the renewed ability to laugh with reckless abandon and feel love in every cell of your body.

Week 47: You're Not Selfish

For some, the holiday season is the most wonderful time of the year. For others, it's the start of stress, over-committing and over-spending.

This post goes out to the others.

I often spend my days teaching workshops on confidence and balance to amazing professionals in and around Philadelphia. One of the things I share in the balance workshop is that even though I live a much more balanced life overall, the obligatory things in my life didn't go away. I didn't find a way to eliminate laundry, bills and groceries, and I certainly didn't find a 25th hour in the day.

I also tell them about choice. Choice is a powerful tool that we often forget. I forgot it for most of my adult life. As we spend our days running around like little whirling dervishes (busy, busy, busy!), we completely forget that we have a choice in the matter. We can choose to do what's best for us.

Making this choice is difficult at first. Some people may be disappointed or confused. After all, every relationship is like a dance, and when you start to make different choices, you're changing your dance steps. Some toes may get stepped on. Rest assured, your dance partners will catch on to your new steps.

But what do you do if the biggest obstacle isn't what others think, but what you think? Are you hearing a little voice saying that you're being selfish? That it's not OK for you to put yourself first or do what's best for you? I know that voice, too, and want you to hear this loud and clear: you're not selfish for doing what's best for you…even during the holidays.

This week, as your schedule starts to get tighter, and your shopping list grows longer, take a moment and figure out what you need. Whatever it is, remember choice. It's probably going to feel uncomfortable, as all new things do, but you're 100% allowed to choose you.

Even during the holidays. Scratch that. Especially during the holidays! Just imagine how much better you'll feel during all of the extra (and obligatory) events if you choose to do what's best for you, even just once.

Week 48: The Magic of Acceptance

Have you ever noticed how people become more or less attractive as you get to know them? The person who you may not have noticed is suddenly desirable because they're an AWESOME human or the total hottie doesn't seem all that great once you realize they're a big jerk. It's kind of magic, right?!

Acceptance works the same way. When you get to the part of a relationship, romantic or platonic, where each person is actually comfortable being fully themselves, that's where the magic happens. When you've demonstrated that you fully accept them – flaws and all – they start to thrive. You start to see more and more of their awesomeness!

What relationship(s) do you have, where this magic is present? Do you have a bestie who has created a judgement free zone, or maybe a partner or relative? Think about how you feel in that relationship versus how you feel with other people in your life. It might make you smile just thinking about the magic of that special relationship.

Now think about your relationship with yourself. Are you smiling when you think about how you feel in that relationship? It is a relationship after all, and unlike the hottie who turned out to be a big jerk, you can't get away from yourself.

Here's the thing. Most of us can clearly connect with the place where that magic is present. We smile and get a warm feeling thinking about the relationship and how we feel when we're with that person. Most of us don't get that same warm feeling when we think about our relationship with ourselves. We may roll our eyes, feel unsettled or simply not want to think about how we feel alone.

So how do we change it? Start by thinking about the magic relationship. What makes it feel that way? What has that person said that lets you know you can be fully yourself with them? What have they done? How do they show up?

Take the answers to all of those questions and apply liberally to yourself! Notice the things you say to yourself. Are you speaking kindly, or is your inner meanie doing most of the talking? Are you allowing your flaws or are you judging them? Are you doing kind things for yourself or are you living a life full of over-commitment and shoulds?

Like I said, your relationship with yourself is the only relationship that's always present, so why not make it the place where the magic happens?!

Week 49: For the Times When You're Overthinking

If I got paid for overthinking, I'd be a rich woman. I'm really good at it, and I'm betting I'm not alone.

Tell me if any of this sounds familiar:
*You're 3 steps ahead of any possible situation
*Unexpected things can really freak you out
*You're the most organized/planned/scheduled person you know

Yup. I'm nodding my head at all of those. I know what it feels like, and I've learned a thing or two about overthinking that will help you reign it in, too.

Sometimes the simplest solution really is the best choice. *WHAT? How can that be? Don't we have to look at the solution from every angle, dissect every potential outcome and make a pro & con list?* Actually, you don't have to do any of that. Like mine, your brain might be wired to work that way, but you get to decide if you want to keep overthinking. It really can be that simple. Next time you find your brain caught in an overthinking loop, as yourself what the simplest solution is, and give it a try.

Not making a decision is proven to be more stressful than making the wrong decision. *WHOA. Is your mind blown, too?* When I learned that, I was speechless. All of that time I'd spent trying to make the "right" choice (ahem, cue the perfectionism!) was actually causing more stress? Yup. It totally was. Next time you're obsessing about what the right thing to do is, just pick something and go with it. You'll immediately feel the stress lessen, simply because you've made a decision.

When in doubt, practice mindfulness. *Deep breaths again? YES.* Deep breaths again, or whatever helps you return to the moment. Take a walk, close your eyes for a minute, phone a friend…whatever your mindfulness practice looks like, when you're caught in the overthinking loop, engage mindfulness!

Most of all, be kind to yourself. A lifetime of overthinking isn't going to go away in 5 minutes.

Start playing with these techniques, be kind to yourself when the overthinking takes over, and get back to practicing some more. Soon you'll notice a little less overthinking and a lot more peace.

Week 50: Let Life Be Your Teacher

Life is full of teachers. Beyond the incredible lessons you can learn from writers and speakers and leaders – there are so many teachers available in our everyday experiences and feelings.

Nature is an eternal teacher. Whether it's learning about the ebb and low of life from watching the ocean, or literally stopping to smell the roses to practice mindfulness; nature always has a lesson to share.

Feelings are one of biggest teachers out there. From joy you learn what makes life worthwhile. From sadness you learn about love. From guilt you learn humility. From jealousy you learn what you desire.

With all of these teachers you'd think some of life's big lessons would be easier to learn!

Unfortunately that's not usually the case. You have to be ready to receive the information and learn the lesson. You know this.

Think of a time when it took you several attempts to learn something. Maybe it was stress management or a mindfulness practice. You probably had a bunch of false starts, despite the best intentions, until finally the lesson "stuck." It clicked. You got it and integrated it into your life.

Did you fail all of those other times? Not at all! You simply weren't ready. Maybe your stress didn't impact you enough to stick with your new habits. Maybe you got really busy after committing to a mindfulness practice. You weren't ready.

My clients often thank me for the things they learn while we're working together. I always make sure to share this Lao Tzu quote with them: "When the student is ready, the teacher will appear."

Take a minute today and let yourself off the hook for any of those lessons you didn't learn.

Start looking for the everyday teachers.

Set an intention to find what you need and watch the teachers appear…when you're ready.

Week 51: When it's Kinder to NOT Stay Quiet

When you get to be an adult, there are MANY times when staying quiet is not the kindest choice.

"If you don't have anything nice to say, don't say anything at all."

Most of us grew up hearing that, and when it comes to playground advice to kids so they treat each other kindly, I'm all for it; but when you get to be an adult there are MANY times when staying quiet is not the kindest choice:
− When you're a leader in a company and you have employees who aren't meeting expectations
− When you're an employee and your compensation is well below market average
− When you see someone being bullied
− When you want to tell someone they hurt your feelings
− When you need something from another person
− When you have an opinion

You get the gist. As adults it's tempting to use this childhood advice as a reason to play small.

Maybe it doesn't feel kind to point out an employee's mistakes; however, the alternative is to let them work themselves into termination never knowing that they could have improved. Maybe it doesn't feel kind to tell someone you need something; however, if you
don't share your needs you risk feeling resentful when they're not met.

There are a few criteria you can apply in situations where you're tempted to stay quiet but suspect that may not be the kindest choice:

1) How will I feel if I don't say something? If the answer is: resentful, guilty, pissed off, taken advantage of, upset, etc.; the kinder choice is to have the conversation.
2) What's likely to result from my speaking up? If the answer is: someone grows, learns, feels supported, gains understanding, etc.; the kinder choice is to say something.
3) What's the reason I don't want to say something? If the answer is: I don't want to rock the boat, I'm uncomfortable, it's scary, I lack the confidence, I've never said anything before, etc.; the kinder choice is to speak out.

Even when it's scary, that doesn't mean you're making the wrong choice…in fact, it probably means it's a great opportunity for you to take a small step towards growth.

Week 52: How Self-Kindness Improves All Areas of Life

From personal change to business growth, for some reason, we all try to bully ourselves into success...and it doesn't work.

When you want to change something in your life, how do you start?
Are you a drill sergeant (I WILL get to the gym every day)?
Are you a task master (I WILL get 5 items on my to do list done by noon)?
Do you use punishment as a motivator (If I don't get 1 new client, NO day off for me)?

How have those things worked? How do they make you feel?

If you're like most people, the drill sergeant/task master/punishment model probably gets you some quick results...but they don't last. Sure, you can bully yourself into going to the gym for a while, but the first day you miss, that inner bully that had been motivating you becomes the voice of sabotage. I knew you wouldn't stick with it. You might as well give up.

LATHER. RINSE. REPEAT. This is the go-to model most people use to try and make change. From personal change to business growth, for some reason, we all try to bully ourselves into success...and it doesn't work.

Here's what does work: Kindness, grace & compassion.

I know you might be rolling your eyes. After all, you probably have lost some weight or grown your business by bullying yourself, but you've probably also realized that your change was very short lived.

Trying to bully yourself into change only makes you feel worse when the inevitable road block appears. Approaching change with kindness and forgiving yourself when you do stumble is what allows you to keep going.

What if your conversation with yourself looked more like this: I've made it to the gym consistently for 10 days in a row. Unfortunately, I missed today because I overslept, but that's OK. My body must have needed the sleep, and I'll be that much more rested when I go back tomorrow. Isn't that dramatically more motivating than: You suck, you're so lazy, you knew you wouldn't be able to keep this up, so there's no point in continuing?

Give this a try for the week, and see how you feel. You might just find it easier to be motivated and continue on when there's a road block, when you use this self-kindness technique.

Final Thoughts

What a year!

Congratulations on spending the last 52 weeks practicing self-kindness, courageously being imperfect, living kinder, and learning some life lessons.

Mark the weeks that had the biggest impact, and come back to them often.

Notice the weeks that were difficult, and give yourself some grace to try them again.

Come back to the practices that called to you and expand on them.

Use these any way, at any time, when you need to give yourself a compassion, courage, or kindness boost!

No part of this eBook may be reproduced or transmitted in any form or by any means, electronic or mechanical, including photocopying, recording or by any information storage and retrieval system, without written permission from the author.

Kind Over Matter (TM) is wholly owned by 929 Partners LLC

All Right Reserved.

www.KindOverMatter.com

62981892R00049

Made in the USA
Middletown, DE
27 January 2018